Heavens Courts
By Brett Connell

ISBN 978-0-9974541-0-9

Contact the Author:
Brett Connell
shiningyourglory@gmx.com

Previous works from Brett Connell:
A Remembrance [2015]   ISBN: 9780986157202

Special thanks to: Jesus Christ, Nancy Connell,
Evangelist Barbara Lynch, Reverend Christopher
Gore, Duncan & Lynda Connell. Thank you so much
for all the support, encouragement and help in
making this book possible.

Table of Contents

Chapter 1: Introductions

We all have great potential as we study the word of God and apply it to our daily lives. We know that it is God that does these works through us, and we know that the Holy Spirit is our teacher concerning the understanding of the word.

We must realize that we cannot depend on our own intellect nor our understanding of the things of God. His ways are not our ways, and it is impossible to fully comprehend or understand God and His ways.

Having established these facts, I invite you to allow the Holy Spirit guide you through this book and give you revelation and understanding of the various points and truths I will be bringing forth. I want to explain something brief about prayer that we need to understand to get an idea of where some of us may be at.

We often pray our desires and ask the Lord to do things for us, whether it be selfless or perhaps something for ourselves. We pray to stop bad things from happening and to have God save a particular soul. We pray for a multitude of reasons, including to end hard trials and tribulations we face. The limitless reasons we pray are vast indeed, but how many of them get answered?

There is a deeper level to prayer that we must come to realize and utilize. Some of us are familiar with our spiritual warfare that we must engage in – but there is a large multitude of saints that do not even understand they are in a daily battle against the enemy of our souls.

If we read and understand our word, God is telling us that we must pick up our cross and follow him daily. Our journey with God is not a picnic. Even the gospel tells us that we will suffer for His namesake. Our enemies will be the members of our own household!

I am saying this because I am about to put prayer in the realm of warfare. We need to understand the truth that our prayers are not simply passive requests that invite no backlash or retaliation. In simpler terms, the enemy doesn't want us 'telling God' on him. Every time we pray and communicate with the Father we are 'telling on the enemy'. This bully, the devil, doesn't like that and plots revenge.

If we are not engaging spiritual forces of darkness at work around us then we are no threat to the enemy or his kingdom. And while I don't believe the enemy will ever 'leave us alone' I do believe he will not resist you as strongly if you are no threat to his kingdom.

I also want to bring up another point up front, because this is something a lot of believers are struggling with. Many have simply not been taught, or have been misguided by corrupted teachings and false doctrines or religious mindsets.

Yes, there are demons. Yes, they can inhabit Christians – born again believers. Did I lose my audience yet?

Let me explain this: You did not live your life in the world as a sinner for years while providing deep trenches for spirits to operate in your life through pain and trauma and then in one moment become born again and magically have all the demons, pain, trauma, soul wounds, fragmented parts of your personality, habits, mindsets, broken heart fragments, generational spirits, curses and generational human interjects leave you immediately all at once with a quiet sneeze.

Yes, these are all real damages that our three-part being (body, soul and spirit) suffers as we live in this fallen world. Remember, the enemy is the prince of this world and the prince of the powers of the air. It is influenced by his usurped authority, but all things are subject to God's sovereignty. The reason I am establishing the enemy's territorial rule is to help you understand that we live in *his* messed up world and we surely will be affected by that corrupted system.

We must understand that God is redeeming and reclaiming the souls of His children from a planet *already fallen* under the sway of the enemy. God tells us not to be mixed with the world (lukewarm) because it has become a system entirely set up for and by the enemy, albeit temporarily. [John 14:30] I will no longer talk much with you, for the ruler of this world is coming, and he has nothing in Me. (NKJV)

Our three-part being consists of body, soul and spirit. Each one has a function and a purpose and must be tended to according to the word to maintain our relationship and journey with God and keep us lined up with His perfect will for our lives.

It is true that a demon cannot *inhabit* or *possess* the spirit of a born again believer, because it becomes the temple of God where evil cannot dwell. Once we receive Jesus Christ as our Lord, our spirit-man becomes instantly perfect – because it is now the Spirit of God dwelling within us. This is the part most believers know of but don't fully understand the finer details.

However, demonic spirits can possess (enter and operate) the body and soul of a person. Therefore the only extent that a demon can operate against a believers spirit-man is to *oppress* (to fight externally, not having direct access). For those who do not know, the soul is your *mind, will and emotions.*

Let the reader understand that spiritual warfare is real and tangible. Witchcraft is real. The forces of darkness, though they do not equal the power of God, do operate on a legal platform in the spirit realm. This legal platform centers largely on the courtroom of Heaven and God's word. We will get into details about this further in the book, but I want to introduce several points about the condition of the Body of Christ first.

Many believers are being swayed by false doctrine. So many of the children of God are told that the Old Testament is irrelevant, and that once you are saved you are always saved. These claims of 'sloppy agape' and 'Christ died for all your sins and you can go ahead and keep on sinning and make it to Heaven' are exactly the lies taking people straight to hell.

The fact is God didn't spare even the angels when they sinned, nor the sinners of Sodom and Gomorrah, and there is no Scripture that says you can continue to live in unrepentant sin and make it to Heaven. We should consider ourselves blessed that God even gave us an *opportunity* to repent for our sins.

Let's just use a perspective of a child to analyze the Old Testament: Back then, you could get the High Priest to atone for all your sins once per year, and you had to worry about angels showing up with swords to kill you for any violation of God's law the rest of the 364 days of the year!

God's grace has carried us a long way since then – can you imagine living in those times right now as things are? I'm here to tell you that there is no license to sin. Taking advantage of God's grace is no different than trampling the Blood of Jesus every time you sin.

[Hosea 4:6] My people are destroyed for lack of knowledge … (KJV)

[Matthew 15:14] Let them alone. They are blind leaders of the blind. And if the blind leads the blind, both will fall into a ditch." (NKJV)

I said that to illustrate the fact that there are many teachers that promote this kind of doctrine and thinking pattern among believers.

The enemy loves nothing more than a church full of "believers" who are comfortably sitting in pews of deception and watered down words that never preach repentance and the conviction of sin. What threat are they to the kingdom of darkness?

But we must also know and understand that there are some God has called to do only a little; and so long as they are obedient to what God has called them to do, and if their heart is right before the Lord they will fulfill what He has asked of them, no matter how little, and make Heaven their home. I am not saying that everyone is called to the same level of warfare, because everyone has different callings and has been created to do different things.

Let us go into the realm of prayer a bit deeper. We must understand that prayer is communication with God. It is not strictly limited to kneeling down beside your bed with hands folded. God hears every thought, every whisper, every desire of the heart, every word spoken and every shout that comes from us.

God is a Spirit and we are made in His image and in His likeness. Therefore, we are designed to look and function similar to how God does. There is no specific rule book that mandates conditions on how prayers are prayed, because communication between you and God is no different than sitting down at your table while eating, or having coffee with God, even laying there talking to Him in your thoughts. It is all the same. Even kneeling beside your bed with your hands folded. Religion likes to put red tape and restrictions on how things have to be a certain way or in a routine before it becomes valid or acceptable to God.

Not one thing gets God's attention more than the other. We must understand this, because God is listening desperately *all the time*.

The enemy would love to convince us otherwise through false doctrine and "religion". Let us get this out up front: There is one God. He is the Most High, and He never changes. "Religion" is dead and God does not operate in religion, because He is One and Truth. It is Spirit calling to spirit, one-on-one between God and your spirit-man inside of you. This is your lifeline and your communication with God, *only* through Jesus Christ. Now, I didn't say 'don't go to church' I just said that the Spirit (of God) is calling to spirit (your spirit-man) and God can speak to you anywhere, not just on Sunday.

[John 14:6] Jesus said to him, "I am the way, the truth, and the life. No one comes to the Father except through Me. (NKJV)

Jesus Christ, the only begotten Son of God intercedes for you before the throne day and night. This is why we aren't dead due to years of unrepentant sin – it is God's grace. However, God's grace and long suffering can shift into tough love if you press Him farther than you ought. Just like any real father.

Praying to our Father in Heaven addresses many of our needs and concerns before the Lord. We can ask Him for many things in prayer, but I wish to share with you some revelation knowledge God has bestowed upon me to share with all people.

Let us examine the scripture on what Jesus said about how to pray: [Matthew 6:7-8] **7** And when you pray, do not use vain repetitions as the heathen do. For they think that they will be heard for their many words. **8** "Therefore do not be like them. For your Father knows the things you have need of before you ask Him. (NKJV)

Our Father already knows what we have need of before we ask Him. This is not a time to babble on about all our wants and problems.

There *is* a time of releasing to God, talking with God, venting to God, laughing with God, being mad at God and not saying anything to Him for a while and then getting over it when you realize it was your fault to begin with, repenting for being mad at God, soaking in God's presence, and many other forms of communication with God. But the time we set aside for serious prayer concerning our deepest concerns should be engaged in a manner slightly different than an off-the-cuff fashion as we can with others.

Our prayers should be presented in a way that works *with* God to see His perfect will come to pass in our lives. This is a place to seek God's face and find out what He wants in the situation and agree with Him, be equipped by Him and have wisdom to carry out His will in that situation.

Let us also not subtract from the fact that our God is a true Father. Yes, there are times God wants us to just cry on His shoulder and spill out all our feelings so He can minister healing to a broken heart. This is not contradicting what we have learned thus far; it is illustrating another method of prayer to be used in different times and seasons.

It says in [Matthew 6:10] Your kingdom come. Your will be done on earth as it is in heaven. (NKJV)

Our function here is to pray along with God that His will shall come to pass down here on Earth as it is in Heaven.

Question: When have we had the power to go to Heaven ourselves to see how it's all done? And since when do we have the power of our own selves to actually do it here on Earth? These rhetorical questions are the foundation of understanding that prayer is time to seek God's face and discover His will and agree with it, and allow Him to guide us in how to do it by listening to His voice.

We want our prayers answered our way and in our timing – we ask believing that God will always give us what we want and what we think is best. And some of us become affronted when we realize we have to do it God's way! But the peace in all this is knowing that God has our best interests in mind and He *does* give us what will not hurt us or hinder us in the perfect timing. Then if that's the case we should trust in God's reasoning and judgment.

The theme here is recognizing our dependency upon the Lord. We like to do things our way by our own understanding and feel like we're accomplishing so much. But if truth be told, we accomplish much more by becoming humble and dependent upon the Lord and utilizing our time to seek Him and bring forth His will into this earth.

[Matthew 6:33] But seek first his kingdom and his righteousness, and all these things will be given to you as well. (NIV)

By seeking God's Kingdom first (and His will in your prayers) and agreeing with God to bring forth His will, God will then turn around and take care of all your needs that you have.

The problem most saints run into is where they pray for God's will and fail to *agree* with it. Without unity and any agreement, it will not be done.

Too often we are "praying" to God telling Him how we want it done, our way, and in our timetable. While I most certainly do teach people that God is a joyous God full of laughter, I encourage you to make Him laugh in another way more befitting a humorous situation rather than making Him laugh with your plans, timetables, demands and great ideas.

Jesus came from Heaven and He still only did what he saw His father do – and He taught us how to pray with the previous scripture. Jesus is saying He didn't do anything of His own accord but only what He heard the Father say and what He saw the Father do.

[John 5:19] Jesus gave them this answer: "Very truly I tell you, the Son can do nothing by himself; he can do only what he sees his Father doing, because whatever the Father does the Son also does. (NIV)

[John 5:30] By myself I can do nothing; I judge only as I hear, and my judgment is just, for I seek not to please myself but him who sent me. (NIV)

Jesus is essentially saying that He only does what He sees and hears His Father doing. He is also saying that *when* He judges it is just – because He only does it in line with His Father's will. Even Jesus seeks God's will and agrees with it to cause it to come to pass.

Why should we be any different? If we are supposed to model ourselves after Jesus our Master – why would we strive to do any less than what He did? Separate from that, Jesus gave us an instruction to pray this way. Why would we desire to be disobedient to this? Why would we desire even to ignore it?

We must take into account each piece of the word of God. Everything in it was spoken for a reason and a purpose.

[2 Timothy 3:16] All Scripture is God-breathed and is useful for teaching, rebuking, correcting and training in righteousness, (NIV)

That means all scripture. The entire bible front-to-back. All of it is God-breathed. That means every word has a plan and a purpose, a function and design to it. I pray that strongholds over people's minds are being broken and any false doctrine and teachings are being burned out as the Holy Spirit ministers truth into the soul.

Also, let us not add to the word what it does not say, and let us not take away from the word what it does say. There is a stern warning in the bible against doing such a thing.

[Revelation 22:18-19] **18** For I testify to everyone who hears the words of the prophecy of this book: If anyone adds to these things, God will add to him the plagues that are written in this book; **19** and if anyone takes away from the words of the book of this prophecy, God shall take away his part from the Book of Life, from the holy city, and from the things which are written in this book. (NKJV)

The 22nd chapter of Revelation does not contain any plagues. Therefore, the book in reference must be a larger portion and not limited to this verse or chapter. Quite possibly, the intention was to convey that every plague in the entire book of Revelation or the entire bible would come upon that person. Either way, both situations would be an incredible nightmare.

In summation, anyone adding to or subtracting from the word of God in its entirety for any reason must suffer these consequences spelled out clearly before us. They will suffer potentially every plague in the book and will not inherit the Kingdom of God.

Let us soak these revelations and truths into our spirit-man and meditate on them. These are foundational truths that we can build upon to establish our faith and wisdom in our walks with God.

Chapter 2: The Foundation of Prayer

Part of our prayer strategy is perseverance and persistence. Jesus taught this in the word many times, particularly in [Luke 18:1-8] **1** Then Jesus told his disciples a parable to show them that they should always pray and not give up. **2** He said: "In a certain town there was a judge who neither feared God nor cared what people thought. **3** And there was a widow in that town who kept coming to him with the plea, 'Grant me justice against my adversary.'

4 "For some time he refused. But finally he said to himself, 'Even though I don't fear God or care what people think, **5** yet because this widow keeps bothering me, I will see that she gets justice, so that she won't eventually come and attack me!'"

6 And the Lord said, "Listen to what the unjust judge says. **7** And will not God bring about justice for his chosen ones, who cry out to him day and night? Will he keep putting them off? **8** I tell you, he will see that they get justice, and quickly. However, when the Son of Man comes, will he find faith on the earth?" (NIV)

Where is the faith of the people? God's word says that He desires to give us justice – and quickly. Jesus did all the work necessary to grant us victory.

God has promised us every blessing of Abraham, Isaac and Jacob. But often times we stumble in doubt and unbelief or we walk in deception.

Truly, we are responsible in many cases for putting the blinders on our own eyes. Many of us have been affected negatively by the average church watering down the word and reducing its power to a canned sermon stripped of all its nutrients.

Many churches negate the Old Testament altogether even though its contents shows the very laws, nature and character of God who is unchanging from day to day. If God never changes then He's the same God in the Old Testament that He is in the New.

[James 1:17] Every good and perfect gift is from above, coming down from the Father of the heavenly lights, who does not change like shifting shadows. (NIV)

[Hebrews 13:8] Jesus Christ is the same yesterday and today and forever. (NIV)

[Malachi 3:6] "I the Lord do not change … (NIV)

We must understand a basic truth that not many people are taught in church these days. The simple truth of the matter is that every time we pray, we enter a conflict. The enemy does not want you to communicate with your Father in Heaven.

One of the first things done in war is the attempt to disrupt communications. This is true throughout wars in history if you research them. How much more will the grand master strategist of evil attempt to take you out of God's presence?

A perfect example of warfare and conflict because of prayer is in the book of Daniel.

[Daniel 10:12-13] **12** Then he said to me, "Do not be afraid, Daniel, for from the first day that you set your heart on understanding this and on humbling yourself before your God, your words were heard, and I have come in response to your words. **13** But the [a]prince of the kingdom of Persia was standing in opposition to me for twenty-one days. Then, behold, Michael, one of the chief [of the celestial] princes, came to help me, for I had been left there with the kings of Persia. (AMP)

Footnotes:
Daniel 10:13
[a] I.e. an evil angel representing the interests of Satan in Persia.

The angel of the Lord came and told Daniel that the very moment he prayed, God heard him, and dispatched this angel to give Daniel what he needed. How many times do we pray and not hear anything right away? Could it be that God heard you the moment you prayed and sent the answer immediately, yet the form that answer will take is being resisted by the powers and principalities that war against and resist us?

The "evil angel" that represented the interest of Persia for Satan was the principality over that region in the heavenlies. There are many principalities and powers of darkness that have rule and authority over large regions and territories. Their function is to resist the plans and purposes of God and to dispatch demons to carry out those assignments.

What is the spirit realm? We all have varying ideas and concepts of this invisible place, but what does the bible have to say about it?

[Colossians 1:16] For by Him all things were created that are in heaven and that are on earth, visible and invisible, whether thrones or dominions or principalities or powers. All things were created through Him and for Him. (NKJV)

This scripture acknowledges that there are things made that are invisible to us, in heaven and also on earth. And that if all things were created through Him then He evidently has sovereignty over all things.

[Ephesians 6:12] For we do not wrestle against flesh and blood, but against the rulers, against the authorities, against the cosmic powers over this present darkness, against the spiritual forces of evil in the heavenly places. (ESV)

This verse talks about cosmic powers. The word cosmic literally means: of or relating to the universe or cosmos, especially as distinct from the earth. Other synonyms are infinite, limitless and boundless.

From these two scriptures we are beginning to see a picture of something that is vast, large, immeasurable and completely invisible. This is in fact the spirit realm.

Are you willing to fight for your answer? Or are we believing God is going to do all the work for us? Daniel was actually fighting spiritual warfare while waiting for his answer because he was fasting and praying during that time!

Daniel was actually doing what Paul explained – that our weapons are not carnal in nature but mighty through God for the pulling down of strongholds. This should give us a glimpse of the type of battles and resistance we might face in our prayer lives. The key is, if it happened with Daniel it could happen with any of us. This is the principle of the bible – the fact that in it contains the things which have happened that reveal the nature of God and the truth and depth of the spiritual realm.

This type of spiritual battle is more of a combat-type battlefield situation. The courtroom however operates in a different wavelength. In the natural realm, you would not behave in court as you would on the battlefield.

The courtroom demands a fear of God and a Holy reverence of Him. This kind of prayer is put in a judicial system as we'll discover throughout this book. Here's a scripture illustrating the procedure Jesus uses:

[Revelation 19:11] Now I saw heaven opened, and behold, a white horse. And He who sat on him was called Faithful and True, and in righteousness He judges and makes war. (NKJV)

The procedure here is that in His righteousness Jesus *judges* and then *makes war*. Jesus gets legal things established and in order first and then executes judgment. It's never the other way around.

Doing warfare and engaging in battle without first seeking God's will for that situation invites backlash and retaliation from the kingdom of darkness. It is possible to step out of your jurisdiction and get tore up by demons. Remember when people ask us to pray for them that you can keep their needs and requests in mind but always seek God's face for how He wants you to pray for them. God knows them better than they know themselves and God knows what is going on in their life better than they do. Do not pray your own will or their will into their own lives and perhaps one day stand before God and have to give account for why you did that.

Now the bible says that Jesus has commissioned us to cast out devils, heal the sick and raise the dead – and this is what we follow as we move forward in this context; however we cannot take this and treat it as 'blanket authority' that covers every single demon, every single sickness, and every single deceased person. We have to have discernment and be close enough to God to hear Him and walk in His Spirit to do the right things at the right time.

Let's take another side note from the parable of the unjust judge and the widow. (We wrote about that earlier in Luke chapter 18). Notice how the woman never once mentions her adversary? She was not on the battlefield engaging her adversary – she was in court pleading for a ruling of justice in her favor. We can assume the woman understood that a verdict from this judge would nip the whole situation in the bud and the enemy would be defeated without her ever swinging her sword.

It would be a very long and draining process to engage Satan himself in the courtroom by our own efforts because he keeps a record of all our wrongs and accuses us day and night. He's the master lawyer that digs up all the dirt on us and the worst part yet is that he knows the word of God better than we do. He knows all the legalistic rules and loopholes and all the laws and commands God has spelled out before us.

We have to enter the courtroom under the blood of Jesus, and if we have any unsettled accounts we should have those taken care of before we go before God. If we enter the courtroom under the righteousness of Christ and in His authority, we will be seeking the will of God and attaining the verdict He desires to give over our lives, situations, circumstances etc.

In the scripture, the woman utilized the correct procedure and the right channel to handle her issue. She sought a verdict from the judge by which she could stand on and have reinforced by the proper authorities. A court order, so to speak, that validated her claims and rights.

To give us a glimpse of the severity of our need to pray, repent and do warfare, let us look into the following scripture:

[Revelation 12:10] Then I heard a loud voice in heaven, saying, "Now the salvation, and the power, and the kingdom (dominion, reign) of our God, and the authority of His Christ have come; for the [a]accuser of our [believing] brothers and sisters has been thrown down [at last], he who accuses them and keeps bringing charges [of sinful behavior] against them before our God day and night. (AMP)

Footnotes:
Revelation 12:10
[a] This is the activity of Satan from which he has earned his name. The activity is most clearly seen in Job 1-2 and in Zechariah 3.

If Satan is doing this – bringing our sins before God and provoking Him to destroy us because of our sin, constantly petitioning Him to pass judgment on us *day and night*, then how often are we in prayer repenting, seeking God to change our ways, and striving to live a Holy life? How often are we praying to cover ourselves from the enemy's attacks and onslaughts? Are we doing this *day and night* also?

Now the bible tells us that Jesus is interceding for us as He is seated at the right hand of the Father in Heaven. This does not "cancel out" what the enemy is doing and Jesus is certainly not doing all the work for us to the degree that we don't have to do anything as a result. What this means, rather, is that it is our job and responsibility to agree with Jesus' intercession in prayer with Him and call those things which He is praying into existence here on earth and in our lives.

It doesn't hurt to ask Jesus what it is He's praying over you so that you can agree with Him and pursue it for yourself in the natural realm.

Is there a situation in your life that you have not seen a breakthrough in, or mountains that have not yet moved? Perhaps it is time to come off the battlefield and into the courtroom.

Jesus Christ is our mediator and high priest – that means that Jesus testifies on our behalf in court. Never forget the Blood of Jesus. The blood is a tool because among many other things, *blood has a voice that can testify*.

[Genesis 4:10] The Lord said, "What have you done? Listen! Your brother's blood cries out to me from the ground. (NIV)

This was the blood of Abel that cried out to God for vengeance when Cain killed him. Even after his death, his blood had a voice that cried out to the Lord. There is further proof of this concept in the bible also:

[Hebrews 12:24] to Jesus the mediator of a new covenant, and to the sprinkled blood that speaks a better word than the blood of Abel. (NIV)

The blood of Jesus speaks a better word than the blood of Abel. The blood of Jesus is innocent, holy, righteous and pure. We must learn to call upon the voice of the blood of Jesus to testify on our behalf in court. The enemy has no power over the blood of Jesus. It was holy, righteous, pure and innocent before, during and after Jesus' death in the physical. At the moment of Jesus' resurrection everything was sealed and set in stone for eternity. The enemy can find no fault or flaw in the blood of Jesus.

In the theme of the courtroom, Jesus is our lawyer. We make our petitions and requests known to Him as He presents it to the Father.

In the Old Testament the duty of the high priest was to offer offerings that granted God the legal right to bless His people rather than have to judge them. In this context, Jesus is our High Priest and offered His blood as the sacrifice to cover our sins as we repent from our hearts. This allows us to stand in His righteousness and be covered in His blood – whereby we can stand in the presence of God.

As priests of our home it is our duty to repent for ourselves and on behalf of our family to untie God's hands and release mercy and grace.

[Ezekiel 22:30-31] **30** I searched for a man among them who would build up the wall and stand in the gap before Me for [the sake of] the land, that I would not destroy it, but I found no one [not even one]. **31** Therefore I have poured out My indignation on them; I have consumed them with the fire of My wrath; I have repaid their way [by bringing it] upon their own heads," says the Lord God. (AMP)

From this passage we see that God desired mercy and sought for an intercessor to appeal to His mercy and grace, yet He found no one. God is slow to anger and delights to show mercy, that is His nature. But He still follows a legal system and He was urging people's hearts to stand in the gap. God needed a legal right (through a willing vessel) to show His mercy towards Jerusalem and even Sodom and Gomorrah.

We see here that one person can repent on behalf of another. This allows God's mercy to come forward rather than His judgment. My hope is that from these principles and examples being brought forth that you will have a deeper understanding of His character and nature so that when you do enter the courtroom you will know your Father and Judge.

If you read the book of Revelation closely and keep the whole book in perspective, the scene you get is God reclaiming the world back unto Himself through a massive courtroom procedure with books and scrolls, the judgment seat and rulings from on High.

We must adopt a mindset that we (through Christ) have been seated in God's presence in heavenly places. It means that through the finished work of Jesus Christ we may boldly approach our God.

Once we recognize that all our works and even the greatest and most genuine things we have done are still as filthy rags before God for He alone is good and holy – the more we are ready to depend and rely upon Jesus, His righteousness and blood.

As we focus in on God's heart and tune ourselves to His mercy and desire to bring His children back to Him, we stand a better chance of being responded to in our prayer life. We have not because we ask not, and we don't receive what we ask for because we ask amiss.

What is God's will? It's His perfect plan, His foremost desire. God has already recorded His perfect will and all the happenings that He desires within the books and scrolls of Heaven. These books and scrolls are accessed within the courtroom of

Heaven – that we may draw upon God's will and pray down His desires for people, nations, events etc. *as it is written about them*.

How do we know that things are written in Heaven?

[Hebrews 10:7] "Then I said, 'Behold, I have come To do Your will, O God—[To fulfill] what is written of Me in the scroll of the book.'" (AMP)

[Psalm 139:16] Your eyes saw my unformed body; all the days ordained for me were written in your book before one of them came to be. (NIV)

Jesus' destiny, as well as all of ours, are written in books and scrolls of Heaven. Now, how do we know that these books are opened in the courtroom of Heaven?

[Daniel 7:9-10] **9** "I kept looking Until thrones were set up, And the Ancient of Days (God) took His seat; His garment was white as snow And the hair of His head like pure wool. His throne was flames of fire; Its wheels were a burning fire. **10** "A river of fire was flowing And coming out from before Him; A thousand thousands were attending Him, And ten thousand times ten thousand were standing before Him; The court was seated, And the books were opened. (AMP)

The court was seated and the books were opened as God Himself sat down and took His seat in the court. And there are many other biblical references to these courts and the books and scrolls which they contain. Daniel had many visions of God establishing rulings and verdicts in the courtroom of Heaven.

If there is one thing the enemy cannot press through, it is a direct mandate from God. The beautiful part of utilizing the courtroom of Heaven is that you are entering a judicial system to call forth God's perfect will to be mandated in the earthly realm with full legal rights and all authority. Once such a verdict is rendered on your behalf, the enemy must yield to the mandate of God.

We have to come to an understanding that our callings, when from God, are totally secure. When I say secure, I mean that God's gifts and callings are without repentance. It is still up to you whether you choose to fulfill that calling or not. God handpicked those He uses before the foundation of the world. Once they were born into this world, He called them and justified them... then glorifies them.

[Romans 8:30] And those he predestined, he also called; those he called, he also justified; those he justified, he also glorified. (NIV)

The process of justification is also that of clearing our slate with the blood of Jesus, giving us legal rights and authority to operate in what He has called us to do. Even this is part of a courtroom procedure, so that we can legally obtain what is written about us in the books and scrolls of Heaven.

We can be confident in our prayer life that God has given us power and authority through Christ – and with all that we have learned thus far, tied in with the holy Scriptures, we know that God has gone through great lengths to provide this authority to us and it is our duty to strengthen our faith and believe as we pray and pull down God's will into this natural realm.

Let us go into some detail about the heavenly realms to gain an understanding of the "layers" that exist in the spirit realm. We will explain the basic concept of this by describing three levels of Heaven:

[2 Corinthians 12:2] I know a man in Christ who fourteen years ago—whether in the body I do not know, or whether out of the body I do not know, God knows—such a one was caught up to the third heaven. (NKJV)

It's an obvious fact that if Paul knew a man who was caught up into the third heaven that there must also be a first and second. In every other place where the bible says 'heaven' it is not distinguishing which one it is. That is left to us to figure out, but let's see if we can describe things a bit better to give more clarification:

[Genesis 1:1] In the beginning God created the heavens and the earth. (NIV)

This is plural. Heavens. Obviously there is more than one from the very beginning.

[Genesis 22:17] I will surely bless you and make your descendants as numerous as the stars in the sky and as the sand on the seashore. Your descendants will take possession of the cities of their enemies (NIV)

The first heaven is in fact, in the physical sense, the earthly realm we exist upon including the atmosphere. This is where principalities and strongmen exist – in addition to portals and gateways to and from other parts of the spirit realm. Our body identifies with this atmosphere and we experience it with all of our 5 senses.

The second heaven is above this, including the expanse over the earth in which the stars and planets are seen in space, and has influence on our soul which is our mind, will and emotions (as does the first heavens). This region expands beyond our universe into a level of heaven that is above our world but below God's kingdom. Here we see very large rulers and authorities operating in constellations and planets, etc.

[Ephesians 6:12] For we do not wrestle against flesh and blood, but against principalities, against powers, against the rulers of the darkness of this age, against spiritual hosts of wickedness in the heavenly places. (NKJV)

These hosts of wickedness operate from the first second heavens. The bible tells us that Lucifer was thrown down from heaven (the third heaven) and cast down to a lower realm (here among us).

[Luke 10:18] And He said to them, "I saw Satan fall like lightning from heaven." (NIV)

Satan now rules and operates from the first and second heavens. This is a great expanse in the atmosphere above the earth but below God's kingdom. The third heaven is the Kingdom of God, what we know as "Heaven" as we think of angels and God's throne, etc. The third heaven is indeed where God's angels reside and is the location of the New Jerusalem.

[Revelation 21:2] Then I, John, saw the holy city, New Jerusalem, coming down out of heaven from God, prepared as a bride adorned for her husband. (NKJV)

The third heaven is also where one receives revelation from God.

[Revelation 4:1-2] After these things I looked, and behold, a door standing open in heaven. And the first voice which I heard was like a trumpet speaking with me, saying, "Come up here, and I will show you things which must take place after this." Immediately I was in the Spirit; and behold, a throne set in heaven, and One sat on the throne. (NKJV)

The voice told John to come up higher. When he did, he was immediately in the Spirit because he then accessed the third heaven realm and stepped into the Kingdom of God.

The foundation of our prayer life needs to be centered upon being in the Spirit and asking God to take us into the third heaven realm when we pray – and close behind us the first and second heavens from operating against us.

Chapter 3: The Power of Our Words

Jesus is the Spirit of Prophecy. His life, His teachings and His heart is the heart of prophecy.

[Revelation 19:10] … For the testimony of Jesus is the spirit of prophecy [His life and teaching are the heart of prophecy]." (AMP)

The prophets of old spoke the word of God as He lead them to do. This is no different than what the prophets do today. The principle is that God predestined them, called them, justified them and then anointed them to hear His voice and to speak what He says.

What is taking place when the prophet speaks? They are literally reading directly out of the books in Heaven as it is written about that person. A true prophet will not speak something that contradicts the word of God because Jesus is the Spirit of prophecy.

While the word tells us to beware of false prophets that have gone out into the world, it doesn't mean that all prophets are false. If you are reading, understanding and living the entire word of God then you should have enough discernment to watch the fruit of people to know whether or not they are a true prophet.

Also just because someone hears God's voice and speaks what He says, doesn't make them a prophet. There is a difference between someone God uses to speak through and a true prophet who operates in the *office* of prophet.

God wants us to intercede on behalf of others and this world to call down His will into fruition. We do this by utilizing the Spirit of Prophecy and praying God's perfect will into situations and even making declarations and decrees. It's not just about what we pray, but every word that comes out of our mouth has power and authority.

I don't think that many of us realize the true power of our words that we speak. I have explained to others that we are always furthering a kingdom every second of every day. We are either speaking words to build up or committing actions to help raise one of three kingdoms: the kingdom of God, the kingdom of darkness or our own personal kingdom.

How did God create the entire universe and all the heavens and earth? He spoke it. His words called forth creation, life and existence. And are we not made in His image and in His likeness? That means we are made in such a way that we look like Him and we function like He does.

Let's go to another level… when God brought a curse upon Adam and Eve. First of all, God gave man dominion over all the land, beasts, etc. We notice that God had all the animals come forth and Adam named them with his words. We can suppose from scripture that Adam's voice was capable of tending to the land and all that was in it.

How can we come to that conclusion? Because when God brought the curse upon Adam and Eve for their sin, notice how God didn't curse Adam himself but rather the grounds ability to respond to his voice – whereby only through sweat and toil would the ground produce and yield it's fruit. God never intended for man to physically labor and toil to produce fruit. It was supposed to respond to his voice and the power of his words. Hence the depth and effectiveness of the curse.

God never took away the power of our words or their effect in the spirit realm. This is why Proverbs warns us sternly against a loose tongue and an idle mouth. This is why James speaks so strongly about the destructive power of the tongue – going so far as to say it is impossible to control.

[James 3:8] but no human being can tame the tongue. It is a restless evil, full of deadly poison. (NIV)

How about what God says about your words? Did you know we are held accountable for every word that we speak? That at the final judgment we will be faced with every word we spoke to answer for the consequences they had?

[Matthew 12:36-37] **36** But I tell you that everyone will have to give account on the day of judgment for every empty word they have spoken. **37** For by your words you will be acquitted, and by your words you will be condemned." (NIV)

When we say to our kids "You're just like your father!" when in fact their father might be absent or in some sort of bondage to alcoholism or perhaps a womanizer – you've just spoken a curse over your child and guess who they're going to grow into? Their father. The devil will make sure to use the power and authority in your words to cause curses to fall on them and allow generational demons to pass down into them to steer them right into that mold.

We have to repent for all idle and negative words we have spoken over ourselves, our children and any others. We must allow the Holy Spirit to tame our tongue and not speak such words over people's lives because it does affect the spirit realm. The enemy loves people who don't understand what they're doing. Here's a tip on how the devil works:

The enemy will try to lie to us and cause us to believe that we have no power in our words, that they are just empty words with no consequence.

He'll tell us that it doesn't matter what we pray or say out loud, perhaps that we're too inferior or unworthy to have such authority. He'll get us believing we can say anything and it doesn't matter.

But in the same moment, he goes before God to accuse us and what is the case he makes before God? He'll tell God to look at you, and the words which you utter forth. "Look at your child speaking all these curses over others and themselves! They have all power and authority in their words and you must allow it and give me permission to use those words to bring evil and curses and demons upon them all".

The truth is folks it's in the bible. God's precepts, His laws and principles are all there. We are warned against our tongue and to speak no evil *because* of the authority in our words. And the devil is a liar – he will tell you one thing then turn around and mock God with the truth.

And this is why our words are so important in the courtroom of Heaven. What we speak forth and decree and declare is something that shall come to pass as we agree with God. We can't forget we are working with God to see His will come to pass. God has chosen to use us to shape how things go in this massive timeline. He doesn't need us – not one bit – but He chose to use us.

When God first started leading me to learn about the courtroom of Heaven, I was severely attacked in my life by demonic oppression. This is something that the enemy doesn't want people to know, and God called me to write this book and explain the courtroom system to the people so they can use it in their prayers and in their walks with God to call forth everything God has for them and for others.

There have been times in deliverance sessions that we have had to utilize the courtroom of Heaven to discover and break legal rights that spirits had to operate in people's lives. We have seen manifested demons shriek and recoil in terror as we brought them before the courtroom and petitioned God to judge and sentence them to punishment.

I once utilized the courtroom of Heaven to petition God to judge this spirit in a fitting manner for what it had done to this person and their lineage. The demon looked at me with pure hate in its eyes and said to me, "You could have been a general in our kingdom. You traitor. You could have had POWER. A general in our kingdom! You are a traitor!"

The woman we were working on was from a foreign country in Africa, there is no way she knew I was an ex-Satanist and have a high calling on my life. The demons knew that. And they know your name in hell, especially if you're tearing down their kingdom through Christ.

I have learned something in my walk with God, that when you truly serve God you have a bullseye on your back and the enemy is out to get you. If you participate in spiritual warfare and engage your calling then the enemy is after you even harder. If you participate in deliverance and casting demons out of people then the devil really makes sure you are fought tooth and nail.

But if you ever once served Satan and participated in his power and made a covenant with him – then broke it to serve the living God, Jesus Christ – and then participate in deliverance, spiritual warfare, engaging your calling – there is a special place for you in the devil's mind and you're the first one to receive the brunt of his onslaught. Your life will forever be harder than if you hadn't served him at all. God showed me this about myself some years ago. But God is faithful and able to destroy the enemy on every side if you truly and fully yield to Jesus. The fruit and reward is so much worth the fight.

It is so important to cut all ties that you or your generational line might have to the enemy. If you want to be truly free from demonic influence and possession/oppression then you need to actively seek and retain deliverance – in addition to seeking

God for any legal right the enemy has to operate through your life and lineage.

It's all about legal rights. God operates on a legal system, and He is bound to it as all of creation is as well.

Have you ever heard people ask why do bad things happen to good people? Has anyone ever challenged your faith by making the argument 'How can a loving God allow such evil things to happen to people?'

Here's your response: God created a legal system by which good and evil operates in; and this is the reason why blessings and curses come forth. Because we are made in His likeness and image, our words and choices affect us and our children, including those around us. Breaking God's rules bring curses which are open doors for demons to influence people to do bad things and it's all legal. Just like it's legal to repent and break curses and cast out demons to stop all of it – if only you believed in Christ and had faith to do so. If you're really upset with God about the condition of the world and the happenings of it – then do what God made you to do and start using the legal system to rid it. The demons are using it, so why aren't you?

So we said all that to say this: there is power in the spirit realm and in the belief and thoughts of your mind. What we fight each day may not even be our fault; but rather the consequences of sin from our relatives being passed down the generations.

[Numbers 14:18] 'The Lord is slow to anger, abounding in love and forgiving sin and rebellion. Yet he does not leave the guilty unpunished; he punishes the children for the sin of the parents to the third and fourth generation.' (NIV)

If great-great granddad committed adultery and never repented of it then you could be walking under a curse and punishment for what he did. You might be addicted to pornography and tormented by spirits of lust and perversion; unable to help yourself because of this sin that occurred back in the generational line.

Is it hard to believe that children are punished for the sins of the parents? Many people would call God cruel for allowing this – even saying in His word that He will do this on purpose. But if you want to get technical and 'legal' about it, let's look at who the cruel one really is. God commanded us to obey His laws, precepts and commands. He commanded us to love Him and each other. Is that too much to ask from the One who sent His only Son to take your place and die on a cross, so that you wouldn't have to, and could make it into Heaven? The fact that we sin even one time makes us the cruel ones, deserving of death and hell. Who are we to hold God to our corrupted moral standards? Let's not forget which one is the Creator and which one is created, here.

Often times people want to get mad at God and accuse Him for allowing something to happen or not allowing something to happen. Either way, people just aren't happy and don't understand and when they are either unwilling or unable to point the finger at themselves, they point it at God.

If only people could see that God doesn't go against our free will and even weeps bitterly at many of the choices we make each day – not wanting these dark roads and deadly choices for people. The hard truth is, God's word is available to us and we have all the power and authority in Christ to stop the curses, sin, evil and death from chugging down our family line. We just never submit to God or believe His word. And hence the enemy runs roughshod over us laughing at us the entire time.

But I am here to tell you that there is something that can be done about this, and we don't have to needlessly suffer at the hands of the enemy. We have some background on how things work, but now we need to dive into the meat of the Courtroom material. Let's establish the procedure for taking care of business in Heaven's Courts.

Chapter 4: The Procedure for Court

The Lord showed me many things about the courtroom of Heaven, and while I do not ritualize anything or believe in cookie-cutter templates to prayer – I did receive a very specific set of instructions on preparing to enter the Courtroom and procedures to follow while presenting ourselves before the Lord.

Always remember that the Holy Spirit is the one that leads, guides and directs in any prayer session. Holy Spirit can lead you to change or pray differently at any time for any reason, but what I am going to show you is what the Lord showed me and I have used this prayer as a framework rather than a ritual – allowing the Holy Spirit to flow as He desires.

Before you make petitions in the courtroom of Heaven, you first need to establish what it is that you want to contend for, intercede for or present before the Lord.

It helps to write down your desires and the things you're seeking for beforehand and then come to the Lord in prayer and have everything ready – just as you would in a real court case. You don't want to go flippantly and unprepared, as you might miss something that you wanted to say or establish.

The next important thing is to search and study the word of God for any scripture or example that reinforces your need or situation. God can't go against His word and He is also faithful to His word – if you use the word as the backbone of your case there isn't anything the enemy can do to refute it.

We begin by inviting the Holy Spirit into the prayer session allowing Him to lead, guide and direct. This ensures that His Spirit is present and guiding us how to pray.

Next we need to present ourselves before God and make ourselves right with Him, and any prayer partner we have also. Even if we are praying alone, we should invite the Holy Spirit to be our prayer partner.

In making ourselves right with God, we are confessing any sin in our lives and any area where we know we are lacking in faithfulness or holding out on God. We must also let any ought go that we have against a brother or sister before coming to the Lord to petition or intercede.

We have to have true repentance, commitment and obedience follow what we say and do in order for God to honor our heart.

Wherever you are praying – seal the room in a box of the blood of Jesus Christ. Draw a bloodline of the Lord Jesus Christ around about you, or over the threshold of the doorway, etc. Call upon the holy angels to fill the room and bind any lingering or territorial strongmen, ruler spirits, power demons, evil spirits, etc. and cover any cursed object that might be in that room in the blood of Jesus Christ and forbid any darkness to operate within the confines of the room.

Use the key of David to close all doors, gates, portals and windows that lead to and from hell. Decree an open portal that leads to the third heaven and that all things must be channeled through this portal.

Also decree the room in which you are in to be set apart for God during the duration of the prayer session. If possible or feasible, anoint or consecrate the room in Jesus' name with oil. If it's not feasible to use oil just speak it forth and decree it. Remember, it is your faith at work.

You also want to decree a fog of the glory of God within the room – to blind, deafen and prevent the enemy from intercepting or interfering in any way, shape or form. Seal all communication and transportation lines in the blood of Jesus Christ.

Pray against any astral projection by cutting the silver cord that demons use to connect human spirit with soul. Bind the demons that connect those cords and release angels to arrest and bind any human spirit astral traveling as well as demons.

Release the breakthrough angels ahead of you to pierce through the first and second heavens, engaging every demonic power and principality in warfare to see your prayer and intercession through to the third heavens as well as any revelation, wisdom or answers God provides to have a clear path back to you through the heavenlies.

I know this sounds "involved" but I say this because of Daniel and how the answer to his prayer and petition was held up in the heavenlies for 21 days by demonic principalities.

Finally, ask for the Holy Spirit to be your mouthpiece and witness. Ask Jesus to mediate on your behalf and approach the throne of grace boldly to enter the courtroom of Heaven.

At this juncture let's review what we have done thus far. We have prepared ourselves where we are at to get things in order in the spirit realm. Really and truly there is power in your words and if you apply your faith to what you say and believe in the authority you have in Christ, everything you speak forth can move heaven and earth. You can move and shift entire spiritual landscapes with your words and your faith.

Satan shudders at the believer who prays and believes. He recoils in fear at the believer who knows their authority and speaks forth the kingdom of God into their lives and upon the earth. But he trembles in abject terror at the believer full of the Spirit who actively engages in warfare against his kingdom with all power and authority – operating in the Spirit of God utilizing every weapon and tool of Heaven.

Satan has no power and no authority other than what you have given to him by allowing him to steal, kill and destroy. He's a tough bully that doesn't back down or quit but if you have Jesus Christ in you then he is under your feet – so long as it is Jesus living in you and not your flesh. Jesus gave you every bit of power and authority He has. So then get deliverance, break generational curses, stop living in sin and be holy as God is holy and destroy the enemy of your soul.

Use your creativity and imagination and speak forth decrees and declarations that are lined up with the word of God. No, you don't have to quote scripture all the time. Speak forth what is in tune with the precepts of God and use the gifts and abilities God gave you to be creative and speak forth other forms of spiritual warfare.

Speak forth fiery swords into existence and pierce demons with them around about you. Speak forth liquid fire from Heaven to fall upon the heads of the evil spirits that operate in witchcraft against you. Return the damage back to them one hundred fold. Speak it forth, and believe it! The demons hate believers with authority who are creative and bold like their Father in Heaven.

I am saying this all to teach you that if you can think it and believe it, you can create it in the spirit realm. Apply this principle to your warfare and your prayers while being led by the Spirit of God. If you open up yourself and allow God to flow freely, you will see much more effectiveness and fruits being produced in your prayers. The more we stuff God in a box the less He can operate in and through us.

Once we have prepared our surroundings and entered the courtroom of Heaven we need to have our case ready and make our claims and petitions before the Lord. There may be specific requests that you have regarding your situation. It is important to be very thorough and specific in what you're asking and seeking for, as the word tells us we have not because we ask not.

Make sure that your requests aren't contradicting God's word or his laws, as He can't do anything for you in those instances.

It is important to note that any time you enter the courtroom of Heaven the enemy of your soul could very well be there to shoot down and refute anything you say or request. This is why we must always use the word of God in our petitions and requests. Satan cannot refute or stand against the word of God – and if we find scripture that fully backs up our petitions and requests, the enemy has no ground to stand on.

God wants us to contend with Him and even remind Him of His promises to us and all the things He has spoken to us in our lifetime. It's not that God has forgotten, but rather He wants this brought before Him by us so that He can look upon us with favor and grace as we petition Him.

Now I didn't say you could commit adultery or fornication (or even not loving your wife as Christ loves the church; all sin is sin, big or small) and then say in the next breath that God's word says you can have every blessing of Abraham, Isaac and Jacob and that you are healed of every sickness and infirmity.

See, there's a legal system in place. It is true that Jesus bore our punishment and by the stripes on his back we are healed. That healing is freely available and readily accessible. Nothing can stop the free gift of that healing and nothing can stop that healing from actually healing you *once it is released in the spirit*. Those conditions were already met and are set in stone.

However, sin is a hindrance and blocks healing. It is the consequence of sin that can block healing from manifesting. Faith alone in Christ has the power to heal our illnesses, but is that power being blocked by a legal right? If you are living in unrepentant sin then you have blockages and hindrances operating against you that stop what God wants and desires to do for you.

I did not contradict myself in these two paragraphs. Nothing can stop the healing from healing you once it has been released by God's divine judgment over your life and situations. But sin *is* a hindrance to block healing *from being released in the first place*.

There is a demonic spirit behind every sickness – and if you tap into the spirit realm and seek God to reveal what spirit it is, you can cast that spirit out of the person and unblock the healing – if in that case it was the demonic spirit blocking the healing and not sin.

Please also understand that God does not bless a mess. In other words, you can't be disobeying God and living in sin while not doing anything about it and expect to be blessed in every area of your life. Every disobedient act carries a consequence. There are curses spelled out in the word pertaining to sin and disobedience. These things still apply today.

No, Jesus did not come to erase the law or cause everyone to escape judgment. Jesus is not a carefree all-encompassing ticket into heaven that clears you of all responsibility and accountability. Through Him you have the *opportunity* to make heaven your home. You still have to live out your part in it and work out your salvation daily.

This is where many people fall short because they can't face the reality that they need to be responsible for retaining their salvation once it is given to them, and they can't cope with the idea that they are accountable for what they know, say and do. It all stems from their character, integrity and nature. This is why healing is a large part of deliverance – to reshape and transform us inside to be more stable people that can conform better to God's word and standard for living regardless of how we were raised or what environment we were brought up in.

There is no time limit on a courtroom session; some sessions I have done lasted only a few minutes whereas others have taken many hours. This varies according to several variables, depending on what Holy Spirit is leading you to do and how big of a case you are presenting before the Lord. The important thing is to not get into rituals or routines. God is alive and always moving – He is always doing something and showing us new things. We need to flow with God as though He is a river and we are at His mercy –

rather than us putting God inside a box and moving nowhere.

You may even hear God's voice while you're in the courtroom in which you can interact with Him through Jesus. It is normal for a lawyer to talk to a judge and for the plaintiff or defendant to hear the judge speak.

It is so important to read and study the word of God and listen to the true prophets of God as well – and also to listen for God ourselves. One of the reasons I say this is because we need to understand the character and nature of God. If we don't know who He is then it affects our relationship. We can't have a solid and stable relationship with someone we barely know, right? So why would this be any different with God?

God is not a robot. That might just be another book title... but God is more than just a loving caring being who we sometimes picture as having a beaming smile. God is everything we are but far more. If you take into account every emotion you have and every feeling you get, you can imagine that God has more and feels more deeply because He is the original that He modeled us after.

Some people get knocked off their chair when I tell them God has a sense of humor and cracks jokes and loves to laugh and have fun. Others run and hide when I tell them that God can chastise you to within an inch of your life if it meant getting your attention and preventing you from going to hell.

This is why we need to have a deep and personal relationship with the True God and not just what a pastor told us or what we read about Him. If we can flow and operate in God's character and nature, we can better understand Him and work with Him. This is essential in a courtroom session. Knowing our Father's heart will help us win a victory in Heaven's courts.

One of the most important factors is contending with God, using His word and boldly pushing His agenda forward in a courtroom session. Having scriptures to back up your case is great but you must also pour your heart into those beliefs and become passionate about your cause.

Chapter 5: Utilizing the Laws in Court

There are some revelations that God has shown me that I want to teach about so that you can use them in your prayer sessions within the courtroom of Heaven. When interceding for others or petitioning for ourselves, there are some mandates we can speak forth. I received this revelation while meditating about deliverances and these mandates are primarily suited for deliverance settings although the Holy Spirit can lead you to use them elsewhere and for different situations. Always let the Holy Spirit lead you!

Here is a list of the following mandates I was shown:

1. WE PETITION THE LORD GOD ALMIGHTY TO HEAR OUR PLEA, WE PRAY THAT YOU WILL OPEN YOUR EARS TO OUR CASE CONCERNING YOUR CHILDREN. WE COME TOGETHER IN AGREEMENT WITH EACH OTHER THAT THESE PETITIONS ARE MADE WITH A THREEFOLD CORD BASED UPON YOUR WORD IN [MATTHEW 18:19-20] WHICH SAYS, "AGAIN, TRULY I TELL YOU THAT IF TWO OF YOU ON EARTH AGREE ABOUT ANYTHING THEY ASK FOR, IT WILL BE DONE FOR THEM BY MY FATHER IN HEAVEN. FOR WHERE TWO OR

THREE GATHER IN MY NAME, THERE AM I WITH THEM." (NIV)

2. WE CALL FORTH A WRIT OF SEIZURE AGAINST THE POWERS, PRINCIPALITIES AND DEMONS THAT HAVE, ARE AND WILL OPERATE THROUGH, WITHIN AND AROUND (*PERSON/PLACE*). MAY THE HOLY ANGELS OF GOD ARREST THEM AT THIS MOMENT.

3. WE NOW CALL FORTH A WRIT OF DEMAND; HABEUS CORPUS - MAY THE HOLY ANGELS OF GOD FORCE THE POWERS, PRINCIPALITIES AND DEMONS REFERRED TO IN THE WRIT OF SEIZURE TO APPEAR WITHIN THIS COURT SESSION IN HEAVEN. IF THEY REFUSE TO APPEAR, THEY MUST PERMENANTLY FORFEIT ALL LEGAL RIGHTS AND JURISDICTION THEY HAVE TO ALL HUMAN VESSELS INVOLVED IN THIS CASE, AND MUST NEVER RETURN TO THEM TO OPPRESS, POSSESS OR OPERATE THROUGH THEM OR AROUND THEM IN ANY WAY, SHAPE OR FORM.

4. WE CALL FORTH A WRIT OF ATTACHMENT AGAINST THE POWERS, PRINCIPALITIES AND DEMONS MENTIONED IN THE WRIT OF SEIZURE SO THAT THE HOLY ANGELS OF GOD MAY GO NOW AND CONFISCATE ALL OF THEIR PROPERTY, OBJECTS OF WORSHIP, IDOLS, CHARMS, AND ARTIFACTS OF POWER.

WE USE THE SWORD OF THE SPIRIT TO
SEPARATE THEM FROM THESE OBJECTS.

5. WE CALL FORTH A WRIT OF COMMITMENT,
    MAY THE HOLY ANGELS OF GOD GO FORTH
    NOW AND DETAIN ALL THE POWERS,
    PRINCIPALITIES AND DEMONS ASSOCIATED
    WITH (*PERSON/PLACE*) THAT WERE
    INCLUDED AND STATED WITHIN THE WRIT OF
    SEIZURE. MAY THEY BE LOCKED IN PRISON
    CAGES COVERED WITH THE BLOOD OF JESUS
    CHRIST, GUARDED BY THE CHIEF ANGEL
    MICHAEL.

6. WE NOW CALL FORTH A WRIT OF
    RESTRICTION TO PREVENT ANY AND ALL
    DEMONS, POWERS AND PRINCIPALITIES
    ADDRESSED AND REFERRED TO FROM THE
    WRIT OF SEIZURE FROM LEAVING THE
    REGION OR TERRITORY OVER, AROUND AND
    THROUGH (*PERSON/PLACE*). THEY ARE
    BARRED FROM FLEEING THROUGH ANY
    PORTALS LEADING TO OR FROM HELL.

7. WE CALL FORTH A WRIT OF FORTIFICATION
    AT THIS TIME TO SEPARATE ALL POWERS,
    PRINCIPALITIES AND DEMONS REFERRED TO
    IN THE WRIT OF SEIZURE FROM SATAN AND
    HIS AUTHORITY. WE CUT THEM OFF FROM
    THEIR RANKS, WE FORBID THEM TO
    COMMUNICATE, AND COMMAND THEM TO

BE SUBJECT ONLY TO THE SOVEREIGN
AUTHORITY OF THE ONE TRUE ALMIGHTY
GOD.

8. WE NOW CALL FORTH A WRIT OF
    ACCOUNTABILITY. WE DEMAND THE
    POWERS, PRINCIPALITIES AND DEMONS
    REFERRED TO AND ADDRESSED WITHIN THE
    WRIT OF SEIZURE TO GIVE ACCOUNT FOR
    THEIR ACTIONS AGAINST (*PERSON/PLACE*)
    AND ALL CHILDREN OF GOD INCLUDED IN
    THIS CASE. IN THE EVENT THAT THEY HAVE
    OVERSTEPPED THEIR BOUNDARIES AND
    CROSSED THE DIVINE LINE OF AUTHORITY –
    WE DEMAND THEY PROVE THEIR
    SUBMISSION TO GOD'S AUTHORITY FOR
    EACH AND EVERY TIME THEY HAVE
    OVERSTEPPED THEIR BOUNDARIES.

9. WE CALL FORTH A WRIT OF EXECUTION; FOR
    EVERY TIME THESE POWERS, PRINCIPALITIES
    AND DEMONS REFERRED TO WITHIN THE
    WRIT OF SEIZURE HAVE OVERSTEPPED THEIR
    BOUNDARIES AND HAVE COMMITTED ANY
    ACTION(S) AGAINST A CHILD OF GOD
    WITHOUT LEGAL RIGHTS OR COMMITTED
    ANY ACTION(S) AGAINST A CHILD OF GOD IN
    A MANNER THAT TRESSPASSED IN ANY WAY,
    SHAPE OR FORM, THEY SHALL BE SUBJECT TO
    IMMEDIATELY RETURN ONE-HUNDRED FOLD

WHAT WAS STOLEN FROM THE CHILDREN OF GOD, FOR EACH VIOLATION.

I have used these in the past in deliverance settings and they have been very effective. People have been set free in the same way that they always were; but they experienced a deeper feeling of lightness and even a return on what was stolen from them. We also found that in the deliverance session there was less oppression to fight through and demons gave us less resistance utilizing these methods according to the leading of the Holy Spirit.

There is truly a boundless area here that we have only begun to tap into. I encourage all of you to pray and seek God for deeper revelation and insight on these materials and allow God to use you and build upon what He has shown to use for yourselves and others.

By decreeing these additional statements you are using your Christ-given authority to establish and institute the law and are giving God legal rights to release angels to carry out these assignments and functions.

If we keep God outside of the box and allow Him to flow and move freely in us – we will see amazing things come forth and take place, and all the glory goes to God.

There are many similarities between how things work on earth and how they work in Heaven. While not everything is the same due to our worlds fallen nature and condition – many things we see here are modeled after what takes place in the spirit realm.

God has gifted you with unique talents, gifts and abilities. He wants to use those in you to come forward with His Kingdom. Each person is made unique with a special set of tools at their disposal. Before we say, 'That's not God!' let's first seek God and see what He is doing with His creation – if it is any of our business!

Let's take a look at a legal maneuver the enemy tried to pull on Peter:

[Luke 22:31] "Simon, Simon (Peter), listen! Satan has demanded permission to sift [all of] you like grain; (AMP)

Satan had to get permission from God in the spirit realm first before he could attack Peter in the way he desired. The same principle applied to Job, in the context that it was dependent upon God's permission whether or not the enemy could sift us or put us in any particular bind.

Do you see the legal premise here that is beginning to take place? And what then was the ultimate reason that the enemy wanted to do this to Peter? It was more than just to serve revenge...

Somehow or another the enemy knew what was written in the books and scrolls of Heaven pertaining to Peter. The enemy knew that if he could get permission to attack and torment Peter that he could try to cause him to fall into sin and keep him in bondage to disqualify Peter from fulfilling his calling.

What is taking place here in the courtroom is the enemy is getting permission from God to sift Peter and then hurls accusations at God related to everything Peter does wrong during that fiery barrage.

God wants us to fulfill what is written about us in the books of Heaven, while the enemy wants to disqualify us with the legal system that he knows so well.

Let's use the following Scripture to illustrate how powerful a single verdict can be in the courtroom of Heaven:

[Daniel 7:26-27] **26** But the court [of the Most High] will sit in judgment, and his dominion will be taken away, [first to be] consumed [gradually] and [then] to be destroyed forever. **27** Then the kingdom and the dominion and the greatness of all the kingdoms under the whole heaven will be given to the people of the saints (believers) of the Most High; His kingdom will be an everlasting kingdom, and all the dominions will serve and obey Him.' (AMP)

In this Scripture, the enemy goes from a place of having the saints in his hands and being allowed to have dominion and rule over the earth – a seemingly hopeless situation – to having all his power and authority robbed from him and is destroyed forever. If you look in the beginning of this Scripture the first thing it says is the court of the Most High will sit (gather together and begin to judge and issues verdicts).

If you read more of Daniel and his visions, you see that the enemy tries to set himself up as God and change the set times and seasons – and that the saints were handed over to him for a time, but then the court of Heaven intervened.

One verdict from the court of Heaven turned the entire stage upside down on a planet-wide scale. So how much more effective will this be for your own personal life?

Chapter 6: The Angels of God

The angels of God are truly one of the most neglected resources in prayer. Angels are actively involved with our lives whether we realize this or not:

[Psalm 34:7] The angel of the Lord encamps around those who fear him, and he delivers them. (NIV)

[Hebrews 1:14] Are not all angels ministering spirits sent to serve those who will inherit salvation? (NIV)

[Hebrews 13:2] Do not forget to show hospitality to strangers, for by so doing some people have shown hospitality to angels without knowing it. (NIV)

There are so many things we do not understand yet about the spirit realm and the angelic host! They are workers who work *with* us so why aren't we aligning with them (in God's purposes) and utilizing them?

[Revelation 22:8-9] **8** I, John, am the one who heard and saw these things. And when I had heard and seen them, I fell down to worship at the feet of the angel who had been showing them to me. **9** But he said to me, "Don't do that! I am a fellow servant with you and with your fellow prophets and with all who keep the words of this scroll. Worship God!" (NIV)

The angel told John not to worship him, that truth be known he was a fellow servant with John, his fellow prophets and with all who keep the words of the scroll. So if we keep the words of this book in our hearts, then that angel is with us, right? And how many others are with us? If Jesus could call upon 12 legions of angels to come to his aid – and we have Christ's authority in us – why can't we call upon 12 legions to protect us in our daily battles against the enemy?

I once saw a vision while I was sitting and praying asking God to release the angels to do different assignments that I was speaking forth and decreeing. I saw a large group of angels sitting in chairs and leaning up against the walls where I was at, listening intently to what I was saying. Each time I sent them forth to accomplish something, they immediately moved with vigor and zeal at blazing speeds – disappearing out of sight to go and bring to pass what I had prayed.

When this happened, more angels came in and descended around me to listen for my words and take assignments and then go and do them. This was a sight to behold and to see the handy work of God in action.

My mother and father have an 80-gallon hot water heater in their basement, and they've had that thing since I could ever remember as a child growing up in the house. It's fairly old, and recently it started having a quirk where it would leak water on the cement floor from some unknown location. Every day there would be a large puddle of water on the floor and my dad would have to set up a large window fan on the ground to air dry the cement.

I suggested to them that they come together in prayer and agree to call upon technician angels to come and fix the water heater and stop any and all leaks. I could just imagine them hanging around their room waiting for assignments and once they speak it forth they split down to the basement with tools to fix the water heater.

I got a phone call the next week to express their astonishment and newfound faith as the water heater hadn't leaked one time since they prayed. The cement floor was completely dry and has remained that way ever since.

In a similar situation, they owned a vehicle that wasn't in production anymore and finding parts for that was downright impossible. And if that wasn't enough, the part number for what they needed was an up-in-the-air type of part number because it was actually two pieces with separate part numbers included in one housing. Being rather expensive, there was no way to verify which part you were actually going to get once it shipped – and they couldn't afford to risk the chance of getting the wrong one as it was non-refundable.

Once again, I suggested they come together in agreement and pray for angels to be sent out to bring the part they need to them. Let the angels do all the work and bring it before you! And lo, two days later I receive a phone call that they happened to come across the actual part they needed for a cheaper price and was clearly labeled as what they needed. They purchased it, had it installed and it worked great.

This all stemmed from a personal experience I had with my wife and my son while out late at night at a gas station. As it turned out we bundled up our son and went for a coffee at a nearby gas station about 10 minutes down the road.

I pulled in, bought our goods and came back to the van to the horror of a dead battery. Now I'm no car genius but I do have every tool necessary with every type of fluid stored in the back of our van just in case. I saw no corrosion on the battery terminals and everything was tightly secured. That battery was flat dead.

After going through my part of diagnostic checks and assessing the situation and dealing with a slight panic, I went into the van and my wife suggested we pray. I came into agreement with her and the Holy Spirit led me to pray for technician angels to jumpstart the battery and cause it to come alive with power in Jesus' name. I got out of the van by faith and lifted the hood up once more, and as I was lifting the engine hood up, a giant massive blue spark arced off the battery terminals (there was no contact of any kind on the battery to cause that) and I knew right then the prayer was answered. I didn't even lift the hood prop up – I just closed the hood and got back into the van and it started up as though it was a new battery.

We drove all the way home with no extra service lights or battery gauges complaining about anything. Eventually, a few months later we did replace the battery with a brand new one. While we understand the power of angels and God's sovereignty, we also understand that we have to do our part as well. In other words, I can't disconnect the battery altogether and pray that God supernaturally provides energy forever so I can save money.

What need do you have? Perhaps you need to send angels into the situation to move heaven and earth on your behalf? There have been many times that I have lost something important and valuable to me, and to many times that I needed something important last-minute and was unable to find it. In these situations, pray that the Holy Spirit would reveal its location to you. Send the angels forth to find it – and you might be surprised by the outcome!

There are many different types of angels. And one time during a church service, I was laying out in the Spirit and saw a mighty vision. I ascended from where I was upwards into the sky. I could see the blue sky and many clouds, but I kept going upward.

I thought I was getting ready to pop into outer space but not so. I reached a point where I passed above the blue sky and clouds and I knew I was no longer on 'earth' but I passed upwards into a new level where there was a second 'blue sky with clouds'.

I thought to myself this is very strange, how can there be two atmospheres? The Holy Spirit spoke to me from this place and told me this was up in the fifth heavens: a place called the City of Angels.

I looked around and I saw wind appear out of nowhere swirling around to take the shape of an angel of the Lord. He manifested out of the wind and did some things, then like a whirling poof he dissipated back into a blast of wind and disappeared.

A similar thing was happening but with fire. Angels appeared and came out of fire and disappeared in the same manner as they came. It looked like they could instantly teleport using these methods. There were so many of them, and they just came to and fro.

The anointing was so strong in this place. As people spoke forth and decreed, these angels were moving about in the City of Angels doing what God had bid them to do. I was shown that we can spiritually ascend to this place and directly speak to the wind and fire to come forth into our lives and circumstances.

What an amazing and invaluable tool God has provided for us to use! The Scriptures even tell us that we have entertained angels unaware. This means there are 'human beings' we have come across that were actually angels in disguise. If you read the Old Testament, angels appeared as men all the time. This still happens today as there are references of this in the New Testament as well.

Chapter 7: Macro Decrees

I was taking a look at some new teachings on demonic structures and ranking systems and I saw some things that interested me. God has shown us in the past that there are specific demons in charge of every curse over a person's life. This purveyor of curses, as God called the position, was managed by a demonic king with many under its authority.

This demonic king would then have the authority to gather as many curses that it wanted and send demons out on assignment to utilize those curses to carry out different strategies against the person.

Here is one demon utilizing an organized list of options available to it and can instantly send out multiple requests, tasks and assignments because of its highly organized nature and rank in authority.

In a deliverance session with someone we saw a demonic spiritual device called "macro vision" attached to their eye gates. The purpose of this device was that one single form of input into the eye gates would trigger an entire list of demonic repercussions and attacks implemented against their mind.

I thought to myself (and really it was the Holy Spirit putting the question inside me) why can't we do that?

What I mean is, we spend so much time praying the same warfare, decrees, strategies and methods that it almost sinks our time by striving to speak forth each one individually. While they are truly effective and powerful; isn't there a way to use Heaven's legal system to make things a bit easier?

The Holy Spirit showed me a neat revelation known as macro decrees. Anyone familiar with software programming will know exactly where I'm going with this already.

The principle here is that we are going into the court of Heaven to create an Article (a separate clause) outlining various decrees, warfare prayers, and other verbal engagements that we can call upon and utilize in the future.

Therefore, when we pray again over our concern or desire, we simply call forth "Article 1" for example, which enacts and releases the 1 hour prayer we used to do – but in an instant.

The process however requires time alone with God and going before Him in the court of Heaven to obtain this legal right to do so. We must have our requests lined up with the word of God and fully prepared and backed up with Scripture. If not, it may be debased and not pass.

To give an example of this, my wife and I were lying in bed one night and she saw a demon move across the living room. I felt the atmosphere shift and there was darkness present. We both came into agreement that this spirit was not allowed to linger in our home – and God began to explain to us how it entered the home and what to do to remove its legal rights.

I immediately anointed the room and sealed it in the blood of Jesus and bound the spirit to the floor, forbidding it to leave the room. In the spirit I saw this demon – it was white, like an albino, and had a huge mouth with a dislocated jaw and huge teeth. It was like something straight out of a movie. It lay there bound with chains and the angels surrounded it watching over it.

I will interject something here at this point that is vital for us to know and practice. I am doing it this way because we have been in a routine with deliverance for a while, but the usual standard is going out the window as God is pouring in new fresh revelation in how to deal with spirits of darkness and I am going to outline this new strategy here, and continue with the result of this deliverance afterward:

I then went into the courtroom of Heaven, asking God to allow me to enter the fifth heaven realm and gain permission to enter His court. I asked for Jesus to be my mediator and the Holy Spirit to be my witness and mouthpiece.

I petitioned God to allow me the authority to create an Article as part of His Kingdom laws (the word of God) and to grant me the legal right as a child and heir of the Kingdom to write down decrees and judgments against the evil spirits that I address.

The following is a copy of the Article that I wrote and spoke forth in the courtroom to be made legal and valid in the spirit realm:

Article 1
The Judgment of God

Conditions:

If the spirit has no legal rights to operate in the capacity which it is acting;
If I (child of God) have the proper jurisdiction to deal with spirit being addressed;
Then:

Judgment upon spirit:

One hundred windows from Heaven will be opened up, surrounding the spirit in a 360° field by which it cannot flee or escape.

From each window 1,000 swords of the Spirit will be released for a total of 100,000 swords. Each sword is coated in the Holy oil from Heaven and set ablaze with the virgin rainbow fire of God.

Each sword will pierce, puncture and completely penetrate the spirit through-and-through – and as the blade passes through the spirit, it will also secrete the Blood of Jesus from the blade.

The swords will also twist as they move continuously, nonstop, and once they have completely penetrated and passed through the spirit they will behave as a boomerang and return to continue the process unceasingly without rest.

In addition to this, a gate from Heaven will be opened to release a bowl carried by two mighty warrior angels of God – and it shall contain the five-fold indignation of God.

The absolute totality and finality of God's Anger, Wrath, Fire, Fury and Judgment will be poured into this bowl full strength. The spirit must drink of this bowl all the way down to the dregs; every drop must be consumed.

The bowl will then be filled an additional time, and for every successive time the bowl is filled it shall be seven times more potent and powerful than the last.

All written judgments will repeat themselves indefinitely until the spirit has lifted all curses, renounced all claims, released every spiritual device and weapon, gathers all of its kind and kingdom unto itself and binds to itself all those in agreement or collusion with itself and removes every part and portion of itself from the person/area/region/territory and goes down to the pit.

Only by meeting this non-negotiable condition will the written judgments cease. In Jesus' name.

Scriptures:

[1 Corinthians 6:3] Know ye not that we shall judge angels? how much more things that pertain to this life? (KJV)

[Isaiah 51:17] Awake, awake, stand up, O Jerusalem, which hast drunk at the hand of the Lord the cup of his fury; thou hast drunken the dregs of the cup of trembling, and wrung them out. (KJV)

[Jeremiah 25:15] For thus saith the Lord God of Israel unto me; Take the wine cup of this fury at my hand,

and cause all the nations, to whom I send thee, to drink it. (KJV)

[Joshua 11:10-12] **10** *And Joshua at that time turned back, and took Hazor, and smote the king thereof with the sword: for Hazor beforetime was the head of all those kingdoms.*

11 *And they smote all the souls that were therein with the edge of the sword, utterly destroying them: there was not any left to breathe: and he burnt Hazor with fire.*

12 *And all the cities of those kings, and all the kings of them, did Joshua take, and smote them with the edge of the sword, and he utterly destroyed them, as Moses the servant of the Lord commanded. (KJV)*

Here is a slight breakdown of this Article to shine some light on its makeup and principles: As we talked about earlier, I am using the authority given me by Jesus Christ and the power of words to establish and create – part of my rights as heir of the Kingdom – to do what Jesus has commissioned us to do.

All these things take place in the spirit realm where the demons operate. We apply our faith (which is the backbone and requirement for our salvation) to these principles and concepts, causing

Heaven to be released and God's Kingdom to advance.

I have found and utilized Scripture to stand on as a foundation for these things which I spoke forth and wrote down – to reinforce and solidify the warfare I am engaging in with God's word.

I stood on this scripture for authority (through Christ) to judge spirits:

[1 Corinthians 6:3] Do you not know that we [believers] will judge angels? How much more then [as to] matters of this life? (AMP)

If I have been given authority to judge angels and more so the matters of this life (which entails casting out demons as part of the great commission) then I have a legal right to establish lawful sentences and different judgments (against spirits) under Christ. Now, I am not saying that I myself have authority to condemn spirits to hell – Jesus already did this. I am doing nothing by myself but rather enforcing what Jesus has already done. The following Scripture proves this:

[John 14:12] Very truly I tell you, whoever believes in me will do the works I have been doing, and they will do even greater things than these, because I am going to the Father. (NIV)

I believe in Jesus and through Him I will do the things He did and even greater things than He did because He now goes to the Father and God has anointed me to do His works according to His plans and purposes. This very same thing applies to you, and everyone else.

There are several other Scriptures in the bible pointing to God's bowl of wrath being used as judgment, and this is why I include it in the Article.

Now having asked God to approve of this Article and seal it in the books of Heaven, I can at any time utilize this against spirits as long as all the conditions are met.

As long as you stay in line with God's word and line up with the Scriptures, your legal document should pass before the court of Heaven.

Now when I engage spirits in warfare in my home, I simply call forth Article 1 of the judgment of God and this horrible form of torment begins immediately in less time than it took for me to say "Article 1" and now I can begin utilizing my time to accomplish other things in the spirit realm.

Afterwards, this spirit immediately went to the pit. My wife heard God say that there were two twin strongmen demonic spirits in our home.

After repenting on behalf of my entire family for any sin we committed that would have allowed these strongmen in our home, we pled the blood of Jesus and broke their assignments over our family and home. My wife and I came into agreement that these strongmen must leave our home – and I called forth Article 1 of the judgment of God and began to command the strongmen to be bound, emptied out and removed from our home in Jesus' name.

Shortly after this, the oppression left and we felt the release. We anointed our home and blessed it and thanked God for all His work in setting our home free.

The time it took to do this warfare was dramatically decreased by this new revelation God has given us. I urge you all to bring this before the Lord in your prayer time and see if God will show you anything new or additional to this revelation and use this in Jesus' name. God will faithfully reward those who seek Him and He is no respecter of persons.

What we need to see is that this revelation can apply to many other areas of our walks with God. This can be applied to our intercessory prayers and other facets of our prayer life.

We are not simply taking shortcuts or cutting corners… we are utilizing the revelation that God has given us to make things more streamline for His

Kingdom. The Holy Spirit is giving us deeper revelation as the end times grows nearer and nearer, because the darkness is growing stronger and darker. We need these tools from Heaven to work with so that we can accomplish the tasks the Lord has set before us.

Chapter 8: The Great Falling Away

We have come into a time and season where we are witnessing the beginning of the end. Never before have we seen so many coming against pastors, ministries, churches and individuals that travel the world preaching the gospel.

I have encountered so many 'Christian' groups that attack one another and put down popular ministers for Christ. I have heard the most wildest accusations that they are secret devil worshipers and operate in witchcraft and black magic.

This blows my mind that people take it upon themselves to assume, criticize, judge and accuse these people and ministries when God didn't tell them to do so, nor did He give them the assignment to expose anyone or their dark deeds in secret (I'm being sarcastic).

It is the job of the Holy Spirit to bring such things into the light, if God so desires to do so. These are things we need to simply pray about and leave in God's hands – not take it upon ourselves to "act on behalf of God". Are you the Holy Spirit? Then we need to leave this alone and put it in God's hands and He will deal with it in His perfect way.

[1 Chronicles 16:22] "Do not touch my anointed ones; do my prophets no harm." (NIV)

[Hebrews 10:30] For we know him who said, "It is mine to avenge; I will repay," and again, "The Lord will judge his people." (NIV)

The best thing to do is if you see something wrong with another ministry to just quietly pray about it yourself and place it in God's hands.

I am stressing this because this is a major part of the great falling away. We need to be focused on God completely and not distracted by the menial things of this world and all of its distractions and ungodly influences.

If your favorite ministry happens to fall – are you going to fall with it? We have to assess where our foundation is, and we have to visit who is our source. I am urging everyone and strongly suggesting that we all get much closer to God and learn to follow the Holy Spirit in every situation that comes up in our lives. We should be walking in the Spirit of God and be led on the path of truth and not swayed off course.

In the book of 2 Thessalonians it gives us a glimpse of what is about to come. Let's look at this as more than just Scripture and picture these events happening in our reality.

In the second chapter of this book, Paul is telling the church in Thessalonica not to be easily unsettled or alarmed by a particular teaching *supposedly by us* (as Paul says) that spoke of Jesus already having returned for the second time. This infers that there were false teachings going out under his name (or those he was associated with). Paul didn't tell them to expose these liars and hunt them down and destroy their ministries. He simply told them not to be alarmed or easily unsettled and reiterated the Truth.

He told them Jesus won't return again for the second time until the man of lawlessness (sin) comes on the scene and the great rebellion occurs. This man of sin will exalt himself above God and even say he is God, with all lying wonders and false signs and miracles.

[2 Thessalonians 2:9-11] **9** The coming of the [Antichrist, the lawless] one is through the activity of Satan, [attended] with great power [all kinds of counterfeit miracles] and [deceptive] signs and false wonders [all of them lies], **10** and by unlimited seduction to evil and with all the deception of wickedness for those who are perishing, because they did not welcome the love of the truth [of the gospel] so as to be saved [they were spiritually blind, and rejected the truth that would have saved them]. **11** Because of this God will send upon them a misleading influence, [an activity of error and deception] so they will believe the lie, (AMP)

Beware of great deceptions and anything that misleads you and steers you off course. If we don't listen to God and His Holy Spirit right now and get ourselves out of sin and be obedient to everything God is calling us to do – then we could be judged in the capacity that we will have strong delusion (from God) enter into us and fall completely away from the faith.

Why would that happen? From rebellion and disobedience to the truth of God's word. In the Scripture it says these people did not welcome the *love* of the truth. In other words, they did not *commit* to the truth. Love is a commitment is it not? It is unwavering, faithful, and steadfast, is it not? So should we be for God's word and truth. And if we're not – then we have holes in us that the enemy can get inside.

I am telling you ahead of time that you are going to see this great falling away and it will affect a massive portion of the Body of Christ. You will see it take place in small increments and it will grow and increase straight into the end times and evolve right into the book of Revelation unfolding before your very eyes.

You are being woken up ahead of time and called to prepare yourselves for this great onslaught. The powers of darkness are being released into the earth with great and mighty power and it is going to take God's glory upon the saints to combat this new and never-before-seen level of darkness.

If we stick with the same exact weapons we have had and used for the last however many years and refuse to upgrade and adapt to new strategies and tools of the Kingdom, then we will not only be outnumbered but severely outgunned as well. The entire point of this book is to teach others how to utilize new strategies that God is trying to show us and prepare ourselves for this gross darkness coming over the land.

How will your resolve hold up when you see so many fall away from the faith? How will you respond to life when the name Jesus becomes a millstone around your neck? What I mean is, when your faith earns you a death warrant in a world controlled by the enemy? What will you do when your prayers seem to fail and those around you stumble and fall? Once again, what is your foundation? What happens when push comes to shove? Can you envision yourself living out the book of Revelation? These times are coming, saints. Will you be ready?

It's alright to be honest and say that you need God's help in preparing yourself to be surely fitted and secured in His bosom. We need to use these tools – particularly the courtroom of Heaven in addition to all our spiritual warfare engagements. We must seek deliverance, healing and strive to live holy and in accordance with God's word.

We need Jesus to move these mountains in a short period of time – and the courtroom of Heaven can help us in this greatly. We need legal rights from the spirit realm to move the obstacles before us and we must actively fight the kingdom of darkness and remove its usurped authority and once again draw the boundary line and push the enemy back across his side. We can fight the devil all day and end up at a stalemate – but a ruling and verdict from God in the courtroom is a mandate that the enemy must obey.

I must stress the importance here that we are being equipped with new revelation, knowledge and tools so that we do not fall into this grand deception and great falling away. This concern is so heavy on my heart – and I hope and pray that this book enlightens and touches many souls and that God's anointing would reach out to you and pull you up from the pit of despair and give you a new hope.

I am bringing up the topic of the great falling away because this is truly something that is not far off in the future. And I am bringing this forward in an attempt to reach out to those who seek a deeper walk with God and who ask their selves if there is something more to God than what they know?

Finally, I urge you strongly to seek God for yourselves on these things and see if God won't give you further revelation and insight into His Kingdom. Never forget or neglect the weapons God has given you to fight with and always keep His wisdom close to your body like a garment and adorn yourselves with His wisdom as you would fine jewelry and necklaces.

By the grace of God, go forward and fight the good fight of faith with all the tools He has equipped you with.

[Proverbs 16:4] The Lord has made everything for its own purpose, Even the wicked [according to their role] for the day of evil. (AMP)

www.ingramcontent.com/pod-product-compliance
Lightning Source LLC
Chambersburg PA
CBHW071829020426
42331CB00007B/1668